A Guided Workbook to Purposeful Living

BY EVA TOBY

Copyright © 2018 Eva Toby

www.evatoby.com

All rights reserved.

ISBN: 978-0-692-08550-9

DEDICATION

I dedicate this book to everyone that I have encountered on my journey of life thus far. The interactions and experiences propel and continue to inspire me to live a life of purpose. No connection is ever a waste. I am forever grateful. Remain Blessed.

........The Journey Continues

MY PURPOSE FACTOR STARTS NOW:

_____ (NAME)

_____ (DATE)

"For I know the plans I have for you," declares the Lord, "plans to prosper you and not harm you, plans to give you hope and a future." Jeremiah 29:11

CONTENTS

Acknowledgements

Preface

Step 1: *Get Clear* 13

Step 2: *Planning* 24

Step 3: *Take Action* 38

Step 4: *Patience* 48

Step 5: *Networking* 61

Step 6: *Your Cheerleaders* 73

Step 7: *Be Fearless* 85

ACKNOWLEDGEMENTS

I must first give All Glory and Honor to my Lord and Savior Jesus Christ for seeing me through. It has been quite the experience and journey over the last few years, but it is by the Grace of God that He saw me through and the workbook is finally here.

To my mother, thank you for your continuous support, strength, and prayers. You never stop believing in me and the vision. I am the person I am today because of you. You have the heart of gold and I am inspired by you always. I love you so much.

To my late father, I miss you so much. Not a day goes by that I do not think about you. And while it has not been easy accepting the fact that you are no longer with us physically, I hold on to the memory of knowing how proud you were of me. It is the belief in me that has made this journey possible. I am eternally grateful.......I Love You Forever.

To all my family and friends in USA, Nigeria, Europe and more, I say a big thank you for your encouragement, love, and support always. I love you all very much.

To my sponsors that made this workbook possible, thank you so much for believing in the vision. I am forever appreciative.

To my publicist Yetunde (Taiwo) Shorters, several years later and we are still making it happen. Thank you for your friendship, love, and support through the years; I am inspired constantly by your drive, passion and vision.

My sincere gratitude to all those that made the workbook come together with your phenomenal talent and services:

Photography: Catherine Schultz-Mia Boudoir (Michigan)
Hair: Yinka Ogunyemi-Omoge Designs (Michigan)
Makeup: Talya Ashford-Beauty Box by Talya (Michigan)
Graphic Design: Sharifa Wynne for ICY PR
Graphic Design: Yetunde Shorters-ICYPR (Miami)

PREFACE

Once I finished writing my book, The Purpose Factor, I actually thought that was it. Especially with the emotional state I was in after the passing of my father just several months after launching the book. I had no desire to do much of anything; therefore, I was destitute of the foresight to even writing a workbook or any another book for that matter.

But I remember getting the message that there is still Purpose In The Pain. That message resonated with me so much. I knew deep in my heart then that was God's way of telling me, I still had more to share about the knowledge and significance of identifying your "Purpose Factor" in order to live a life of fulfillment. Pair that with the support and positive feedback from friends, family, and fans alike that would tell me the huge impact the book had on their journey to purposeful living; and as a result The Purpose Factor Workbook was born.

The Purpose Factor workbook was designed to reinforce the strategies that were discussed in the book. If you have not done so already, I encourage you to read the book, before you start your workbook journey. In this workbook you will find practical methods, modules and activities which correspond to the different chapters from the book.

It is my hope that this guided workbook provides you with more insight and gives you the precision and confidence of uncovering your sense of purpose in order to gain contentment. Cheers to discovering your Purpose Factor...Let the journey begin!

SUCCESS IS PURPOSE ACHIEVED...

STEP 1: GET CLEAR

It is essential to have a clear mind in order to identify and concentrate on your purpose. You may not be cognizant of it, but there are so many distracting thoughts and stressors that are invading your mental space. These thoughts interfere and contribute to stagnancy when it comes to goal attainment. Having a clear mind increases your focus and productivity. A de-cluttered mind is an effective mind.

"BRAIN DUMP 101: CLEAR IT OUT"

Take the next two minutes to write down everything you are thinking about and feeling at the moment.

"A lack of clarity could put the brakes on any journey to success." - *Steve Maraboli*

"PRIORITIZE IT"

Stephen Covey's The Time Management Matrix is a powerful tool that allows you to prioritize your goals and commitments. It helps to identify what you are really spending your time on.

TIME MANAGEMENT MATRIX EXAMPLE:

Source: Stephen Covey, 7 Habits of Highly Effective People
Image Source: http://pasteurtran.com/revisiting-stephen-covey-time-management-grid/

Directions: Based on the list from your Brain Dump, prioritize and assign each item to a quadrant.

"You define what is important to you by what you dedicate your time to." – *Unknown*

NOTES:

STEP 2: PLANNING

Before you can even start planning you must first identify what it is you want to do and were called to do. Therefore it is important to uncover your passion, natural gifts, and talents which can ultimately position you for your purpose. Remember your calling is closely linked to the things you enjoy doing.

"MY ROAD MAP TO PURPOSE"

Directions: Complete the Road Map below by answering the questions.

START
"My Journey Begins Now"

STEP 1: "What do I enjoy and love doing the most?"

What makes me smile? Think of people, hobbies, and activities What makes me loose track of time?

STEP 2: "What am I naturally good at doing?"

What are my strengths? What do others praise and give me props for?

STEP 3: "What makes me feel great about myself?"

Think about your gifts and passions? What do most people ask me for help in?

STEP 4: "What are my deepest values?"

What do I value the most? What guides your behaviors, choices, and gives meaning to your life?

STEP 5: "How can I use my talents, strengths, and values to make an impact in the world?"

What would I want to be remembered by?

STEP 6: "Considering all the possibilities from Step 5, select one that really resonates with you. This is your life's purpose."

MY PURPOSE FACTOR IS:_____

"All you need is the plan, the road map, and the courage to press on to your destination." - *Earl Nightingale*

"THE PURPOSE FACTOR IN OTHERS"

Directions: Below write down a list of all the people you admire; and what you specifically admire in them and their purpose.

NAMES OF PEOPLE I ADMIRE	WHAT I SPECIFICALLY ADMIRE ABOUT THEM
1.	
2.	
3.	
4.	
5.	
6.	
7.	

"Don't imitate others. Be yourself. But allow the people you admire to inspire you." - *Chalene Johnson*

"THE VISION"

Now that you have identified your Purpose Factor, it is time to depict the Vision. You will now create your own vision board if you do not have one already. Vision Boards are impactful tools that enable you to have a visual representation of your goals and aspirations as identified on your 'Road Map to Your Purpose.' Your vision board entails the things that inspire and motivate you.

ITEMS YOU WILL NEED:

- A board cork, framed like 18x 24 or 24 x 24
- Scissors
- Tape, pin and/or glue stick
- Colorful markers and stickers
- Magazines that you can cut images and quotes or sayings from

HOW IT WORKS:

1. Make sure you set the right mood by cutting off all distractions and noise. Go to a quiet place that will allow you to concentrate on this task.

2. Using your Road Map to Your Purpose as a point of reference, cut out images from magazines that inspire you and symbolize the life you want to live. For instance, if you always dreamed of being a singer, you can cut out clips of famous singers that inspire you.

3. Take your photo clips and paste them on your boards. Please note there is no specific order they should be placed on the board.

4. You can then either write with your marker or cut out clips of some of you favorite quotes, scriptures and mantras that motivate you. The sayings are meant to be reminders of the life you want to live.

5. Don't worry if your board is not filled up. You can always add to it and rearrange as various things come up in your life.

6. Now display you vision board in the place that will require you to see it everyday. For instance, in front of your bed, in your kitchen, personal office space, etc…

EXAMPLE OF A VISION BOARD.

"Clarify your vision...plan with precision"- Unknown

NOTES:

STEP 3: TAKE ACTION

Living a life of purpose requires you to act upon your intentions. To live a life of fulfillment is a matter of moving in the direction of application.

"READY-SET-GOAL!!!"

Directions: Set one major goal you wish to accomplish in the next 90 days.

WHAT IS MY GOAL

WHAT ACTION STEPS DO I NEED TO TAKE TO ACCOMPLISH THIS GOAL?

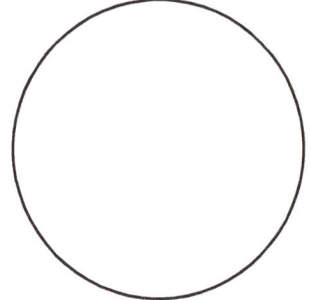 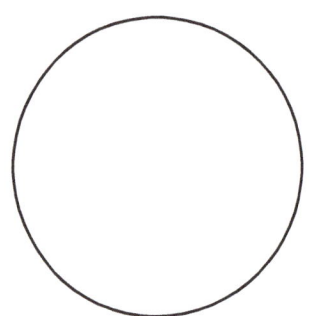 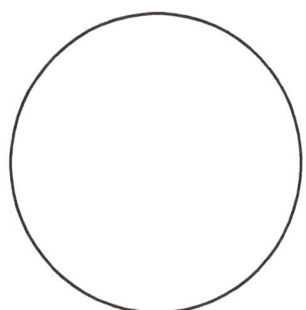

Reaching this goal is important to me because? Does it align with the things I value?

Who are the people that can help and support me in achieving this goal?

DURATION TO COMPLETE THIS GOAL? 90 DAYS

Start Date: _____   End Date: _____

"Vision without execution is delusion." - *Thomas Edison*

"WEEKLY ACTION PLAN"

Directions: Make a list of 3-5 things you will do each week in order to bring your goal which you have identified to fruition.

WEEK 1: _____ (date)

_____
_____
_____
_____
_____

WEEK 2: _____ (date)

_____
_____
_____
_____
_____

SELF-EVALUATION

HOW DO I RATE MY EFFORTS THIS WEEK IN TAKING ACTION TO REACH MY GOAL?

1	2	3	4	5
Poor	Average	Good	Very Good	Excellent

SELF-EVALUATION

HOW DO I RATE MY EFFORTS THIS WEEK IN TAKING ACTION TO REACH MY GOAL?

1	2	3	4	5
Poor	Average	Good	Very Good	Excellent

REFLECTIONS

I GAVE MYSELF THE ABOVE EVALUATION BECAUSE

REFLECTIONS

I GAVE MYSELF THE ABOVE EVALUATION BECAUSE

"A Journey of a thousand miles must begin with a single step." - Lao Tzu

"WEEKLY ACTION PLAN"

Directions: Make a list of 3-5 things you will do each week in order to bring your goal which you have identified to fruition.

WEEK 3: _____ (date)

_____
_____
_____
_____
_____

SELF-EVALUATION

HOW DO I RATE MY EFFORTS THIS WEEK IN TAKING ACTION TO REACH MY GOAL?

1	2	3	4	5
Poor	Average	Good	Very Good	Excellent

REFLECTIONS

I GAVE MYSELF THE ABOVE EVALUATION BECAUSE

WEEK 4: _____ (date)

_____
_____
_____
_____
_____

SELF-EVALUATION

HOW DO I RATE MY EFFORTS THIS WEEK IN TAKING ACTION TO REACH MY GOAL?

1	2	3	4	5
Poor	Average	Good	Very Good	Excellent

REFLECTIONS

I GAVE MYSELF THE ABOVE EVALUATION BECAUSE

"The path to success is to take massive determined actions." - Tony Robbins

"WEEKLY ACTION PLAN"

Directions: Make a list of 3-5 things you will do each week in order to bring your goal which you have identified to fruition.

WEEK 5: _____ (date)

_____
_____
_____
_____
_____

WEEK 6: _____ (date)

_____
_____
_____
_____
_____

SELF-EVALUATION
HOW DO I RATE MY EFFORTS THIS WEEK IN TAKING ACTION TO REACH MY GOAL?
1 Poor   2 Average   3 Good   4 Very Good   5 Excellent

SELF-EVALUATION
HOW DO I RATE MY EFFORTS THIS WEEK IN TAKING ACTION TO REACH MY GOAL?
1 Poor   2 Average   3 Good   4 Very Good   5 Excellent

REFLECTIONS
I GAVE MYSELF THE ABOVE EVALUATION BECAUSE

REFLECTIONS
I GAVE MYSELF THE ABOVE EVALUATION BECAUSE

"Action is the foundational key to all success." - *Pablo Picaso*

"WEEKLY ACTION PLAN"

Directions: Make a list of 3-5 things you will do each week in order to bring your goal which you have identified to fruition.

WEEK 7: _____(date)

_____
_____
_____
_____
_____

WEEK 8: _____(date)

_____
_____
_____
_____
_____

SELF-EVALUATION
HOW DO I RATE MY EFFORTS THIS WEEK IN TAKING ACTION TO REACH MY GOAL?
1 — Poor   2 — Average   3 — Good   4 — Very Good   5 — Excellent

SELF-EVALUATION
HOW DO I RATE MY EFFORTS THIS WEEK IN TAKING ACTION TO REACH MY GOAL?
1 — Poor   2 — Average   3 — Good   4 — Very Good   5 — Excellent

REFLECTIONS
I GAVE MYSELF THE ABOVE EVALUATION BECAUSE

REFLECTIONS
I GAVE MYSELF THE ABOVE EVALUATION BECAUSE

"Dream Big. Set Goals. Take Action." –Unknown

"WEEKLY ACTION PLAN"

Directions: Make a list of 3-5 things you will do each week in order to bring your goal which you have identified to fruition.

WEEK 9: _____(date)

_____
_____
_____
_____
_____

WEEK 10: _____(date)

_____
_____
_____
_____
_____

SELF-EVALUATION
HOW DO I RATE MY EFFORTS THIS WEEK IN TAKING ACTION TO REACH MY GOAL?
1   2   3   4   5   Poor   Average   Good   Very Good   Excellent

SELF-EVALUATION
HOW DO I RATE MY EFFORTS THIS WEEK IN TAKING ACTION TO REACH MY GOAL?
1   2   3   4   5   Poor   Average   Good   Very Good   Excellent

REFLECTIONS
I GAVE MYSELF THE ABOVE EVALUATION BECAUSE

REFLECTIONS
I GAVE MYSELF THE ABOVE EVALUATION BECAUSE

"It is action that creates motivation." – *Steve Backley*

"WEEKLY ACTION PLAN"

Directions: Make a list of 3-5 things you will do each week in order to bring your goal which you have identified to fruition.

WEEK 11: _____(date)

_____
_____
_____
_____
_____

WEEK 12: _____(date)

_____
_____
_____
_____
_____

SELF-EVALUATION
HOW DO I RATE MY EFFORTS THIS WEEK IN TAKING ACTION TO REACH MY GOAL?
1 — Poor 2 — Average 3 — Good 4 — Very Good 5 — Excellent

SELF-EVALUATION
HOW DO I RATE MY EFFORTS THIS WEEK IN TAKING ACTION TO REACH MY GOAL?
1 — Poor 2 — Average 3 — Good 4 — Very Good 5 — Excellent

REFLECTIONS
I GAVE MYSELF THE ABOVE EVALUATION BECAUSE

REFLECTIONS
I GAVE MYSELF THE ABOVE EVALUATION BECAUSE

"Goals are dreams we convert to plans and take action to fulfill." - *Zig Ziglar*

NOTES:

STEP 4: PATIENCE

In the process of attaining your goals and purpose, it is essential to cultivate patience. Success does not happen overnight. Therefore, in order to be successful we need patience. Just like crops need time to grow and harvest after the seeds have been planted, the same applies for the time you need in attaining your goals. If you become impatient in pursuit of your goals, you may become discouraged and quit. You have to be able to water and nurture your goals with diligence, discipline, and determination so that those goals become a reality.

"MY PATIENCE"

Directions: Fill out the following items as it relates to your Patience.

WHAT DOES PATIENCE MEAN TO YOU:

DO YOU CONSIDER YOURSELF A PATIENT PERSON?   CIRCLE: YES   NO   MAYBE

EXPLAIN:

"Patience is not the ability to wait but how you act while you are waiting." - *Joyce Meyers*

I HAVE FOUND MYSELF BEING PATIENT WHEN...

A. _____
B. _____
C. _____
D. _____
E. _____
F. _____

CIRCUMSTANCES THAT TRIGGER MY IMPATIENCE....

A. _____
B. _____
C. _____
D. _____
E. _____
F. _____

WHAT ARE SOME SIGNS/SYMPTOMS OF IMPATIENCE (PERSONAL/GENERAL):

I CAN SHOW PATIENCE BY DOING THE FOLLOWING:

"Stay patient and trust the journey."- *Unknown*

Directions: Write in the hour glass all your goals you wish to accomplish over a period of time.

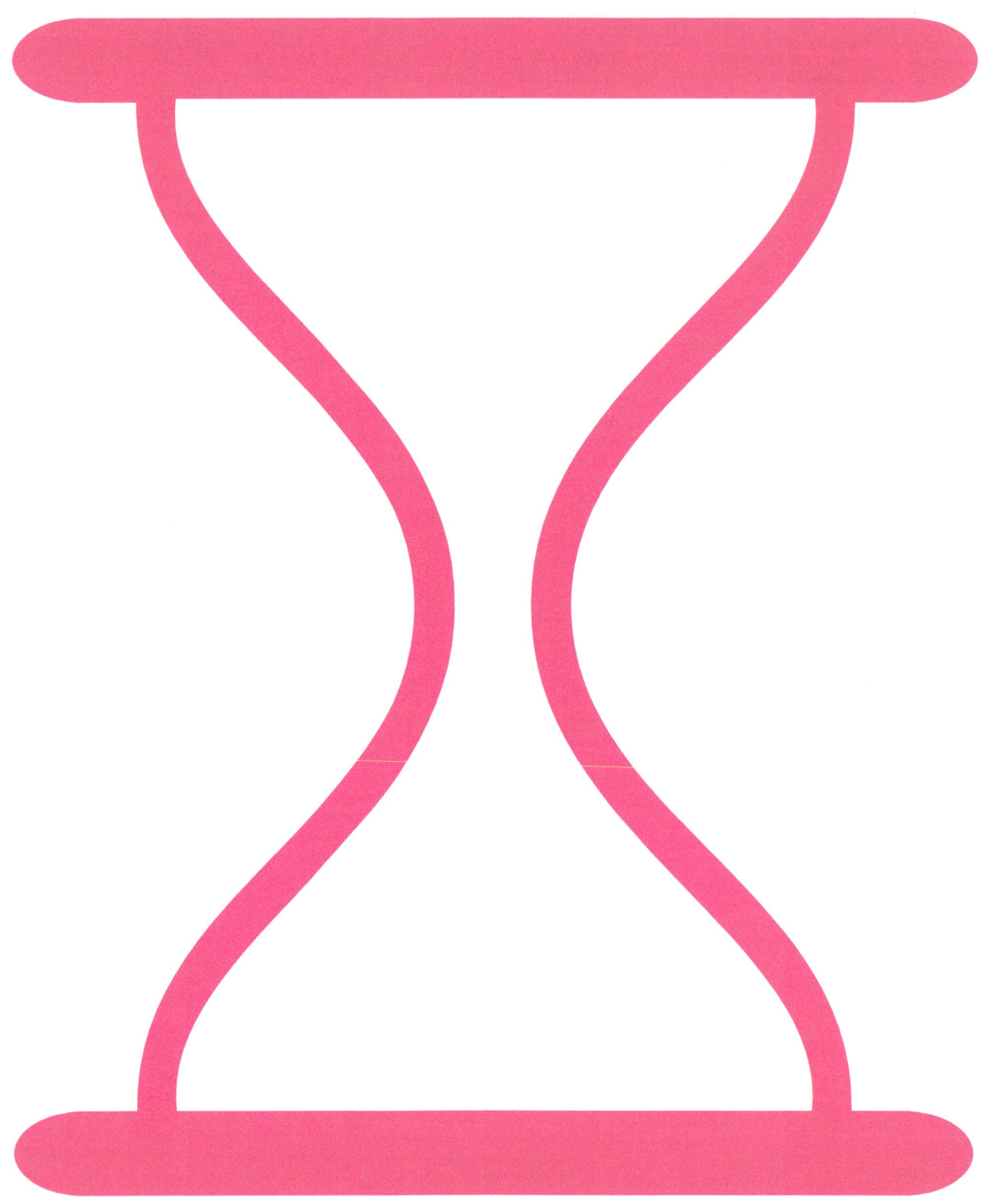

"Patience is not a passive waiting. Patience is active acceptance of the process required to attaining your goals and dreams."- *Ray Davis*

NOTES:

STEP 5: NETWORKING

While networking can seem like a daunting and intimidating task, it is actually a powerful exchange that can connect you to essential resources and people on your purposeful journey. No connection is ever wasted, therefore, you want to position yourself and be open for opportunities.

"MY 30-DAY NAP" (Networking Action Plan)

Directions: For the next 30 days challenge yourself and put together your own Networking Action Plan. Remember it is all about making connections. The goal here is to engage in a networking activity each day. You can fill out your calendar based on the suggested networking activities listed below.

SUN	MON	TUES	WED	THURS	FRI	SAT

"If you want to go fast go alone. If you want to go far go with others."- African Proverb

NETWORKING ACTIVITIES:

- Clearly identify what my goals are for this month.
- Make a list of the types of people currently in my network.
- Identify people in my network that I want to learn more about.
- Call or email at least two people in my network that I want to learn more about.
- Request to have meeting (informational interview) with those people in my network.
- Make a list of questions to ask during my informational interview (the purpose of this meeting is to ask them about their careers/professions, and pick their brain of sorts.)
- Pick out an interview outfit. If I were called for a business meeting would I be ready?
- Research local events I can attend that are targeted to my goals and pursuits.
- Attend a networking event and meet at least two people I do not know.
- Volunteer and participate in a community outreach project I.e. Neighborhood cleanup, feed homeless, etc..
- Mastering the art of small talk, come up with some conversation starters. I.e. commonality, current events, etc...
- Obtain contact information and follow-up with the individuals I met at networking event.
- Attend a social gathering and meet at least three people and find out three things we have in common.
- Make a list of friends, former colleagues, and/or business contacts I would like to reconnect with.
- Be generous...Think about ways I can help someone in my network.
- Join my college alumni association and research upcoming activities and events.

- Join a professional organization targeted to my career/industry.
- Create a LinkedIn account and profile.
- Create and update my resume.
- Create a business card.
- Try a new hobby or social activity to meet new people.
- Plan to go out to lunch with an acquaintance, colleague or neighbor I don't know very well.
- Send LinkedIn requests to the people I have been meeting through my networking this month.
- Make a networking log of all those I have made connections with during this month of networking.
- Write down what I have learned about these individuals.
- Follow up with the connections I have met thus far and thank them for their time.
- Identify an accountability partner to hold me accountable for completing my NAP.
- Review my goal with my accountability partner to assure I am on the right track.
- Keep a journal of my daily progress.
- VICTORY celebration!! I completed my 30day NAP!!! Treat myself to something nice for job well done.

"No connection is ever a waste." – *Unknown*

NOTES:

STEP 6: YOUR CHEERLEADERS

Having the determination and ambition to reach your goal is one thing, but having cheerleaders is an essential element on your purposeful journey to success. Your cheerleaders are your steadfast partners in purpose. They affirm your value and hold you accountable to keep moving in the direction of your goals. Nobody said the road to success will be easy. There will be several days along your journey when your emotional strength and motivation is tested; But this is why your cheerleaders are so imperative. Your cheerleaders are secure in their function by affirming your efforts and propelling you to stay the course.

"ESTABLISHING YOUR CHEERLEADERS"

Directions: Identify at least one positive cheerleader in each area of your life.

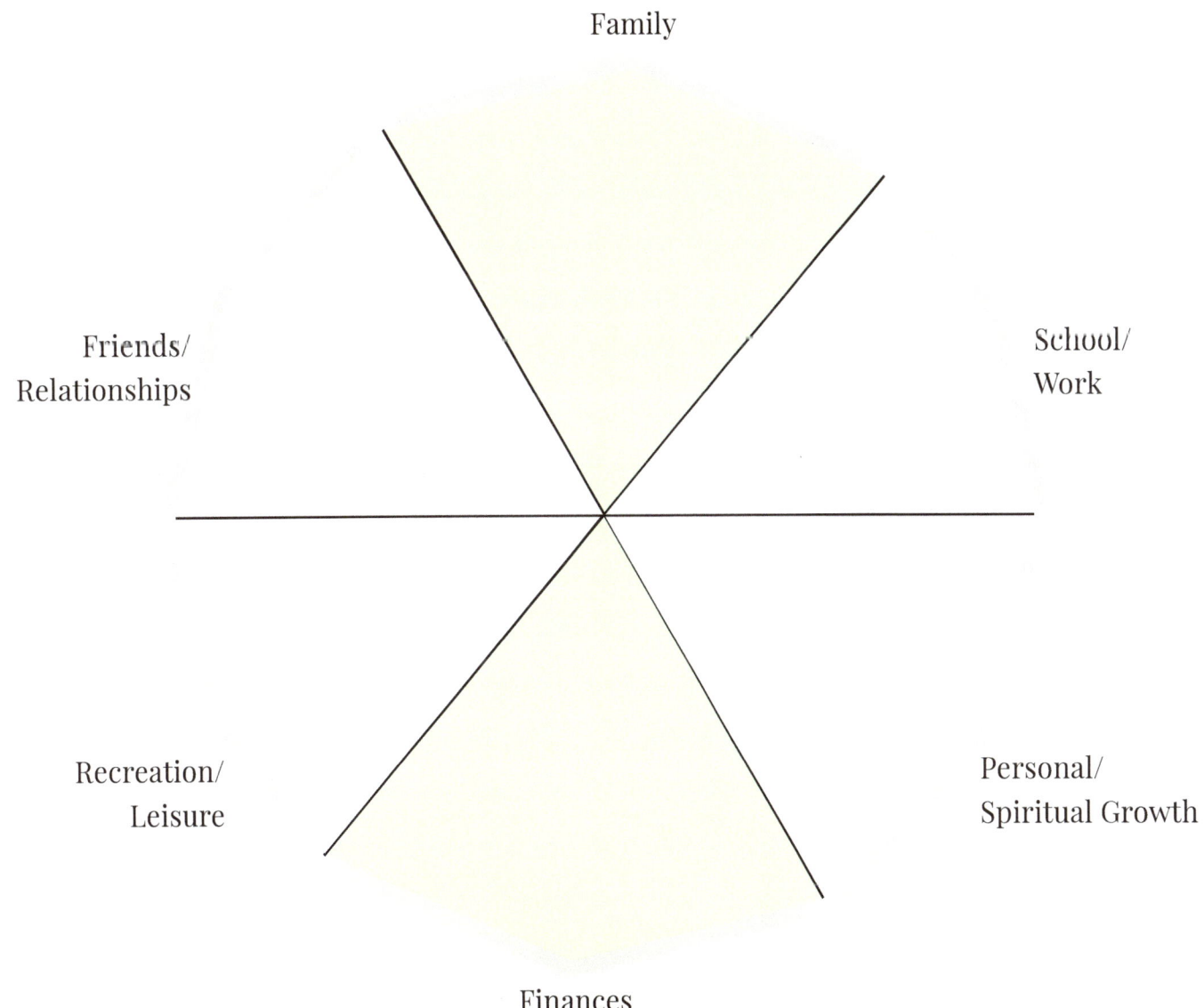

"Surround yourself only with people who are going to lift you higher." - *Oprah Winfrey*

"MY CHEERLEADER TREE"

Directions: Complete your tree of support by making a list of names and determine who is most likely to assist you in the following situations.

Most likely to tell me the truth:
_____

Most likely to motivate me:
_____

Most likely to still support me a year from now:
_____

The best listener:
_____

Most likely to not pass judgment:
_____

Most likely to notice if I am not having a good day:
_____

Most likely to give me good advice:
_____

"It is amazing how far you can go, just because someone believed in you." - *GBatiste*

NOTES:

STEP 7: BE FEARLESS

In order to create the life of your dreams you have to step out on faith and be fearless. Faith and fear cannot coexist in the same realm. Eventually one is going to win. Fear can be breeding ground to stagnancy. Do not be tempted to take up the parking spaces of fear along your journey to success. Therefore, it is imperative to break through the barrier of fear in order to embrace your destiny and purpose-filled life.

"MY FEARLESS JOURNEY"

Directions: Write down one goal and in the parking spaces, list the different barriers of fear that are preventing you from reaching that goal.

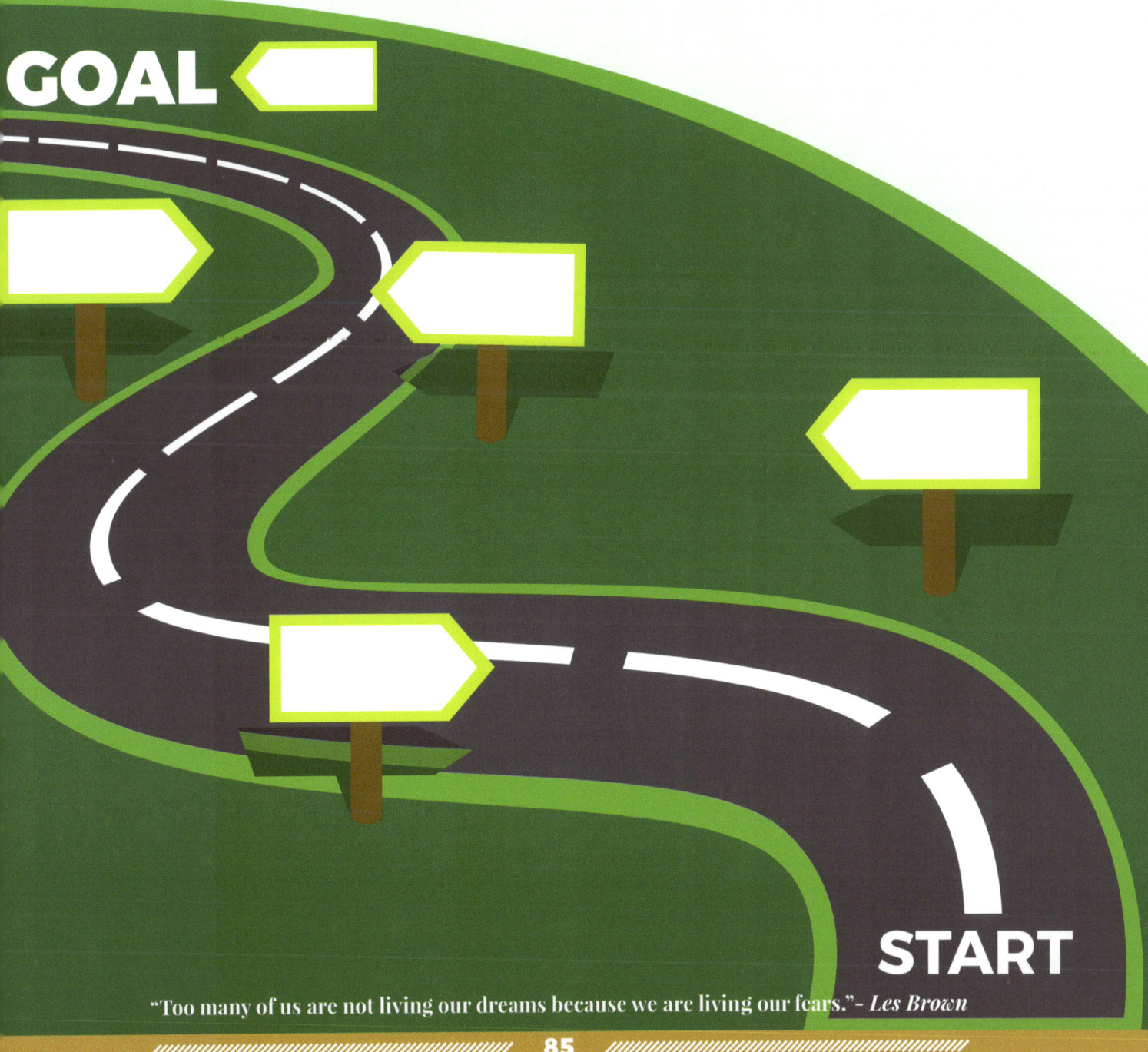

"Too many of us are not living our dreams because we are living our fears." - *Les Brown*

"MY FEARLESS BREAKTHROUGH"

Directions: Based on the barriers of fear you identified in your parking spaces, list what you can do to breakthrough those barriers and be fearless!!!!!

"Once you become fearless life becomes limitless."- Unknown

NOTES:

ABOUT THE AUTHOR

Eva is a bestselling author and natural enthusiast when it comes to living a life of purpose. Growing up as a Nigerian-American, at an early age Eva's intelligent and ambitious disposition has always made her standout. Eva graduated from the University of Michigan (Ann Arbor) with a Bachelor's degree in Psychology, and Master's degree in Social Work, respectively; and graduated with a Master's degree in Business Administration (MBA) from Eastern Michigan University. As an entrepreneur, Eva has a passion for motivating people to maximize their full potential and develop a sense of purpose.

As a Michigan native, Eva began her career working as a social worker and social worker consultant/trainer for the State of Michigan. Eva also worked as a licensed clinical therapist. Eva eventually transitioned into other pursuits full-time which included being a presenter/spokesmodel for prominent global brands like Chrysler and General Motors. Eva has also served as a motivational and keynote speaker for several educational, religious, non-profit, and business organizations.

YOUR PURPOSE FACTOR WORKBOOK EXPERIENCE......

I would like to take this opportunity to express my sincere gratitude for the purchase of this workbook and supporting me on this Purpose Factor journey. My hope is that you gained more insight and knowledge about strategies to purposeful living. Just like the book, your review would be greatly appreciated. Additionally, if you consider it was of value, please feel free to share your views with your friends, family, and fans on your social media platforms. Let us continue to inspire others to Live with Purpose....Remain Blessed Always.

CONNECT WITH EVA TOBY:

 @evatoby    Eva Toby    EvaTobyTV   EvaTobyXE

WWW.EVATOBY.COM

SO WHAT DID YOU THINK? HEAD OVER TO AMAZON.COM AND LEAVE A REVIEW.

Let me and the world know what you thought about this workbook and how you used it. I look forward to your review. I appreciate you taking the time.

Thank you.

Sincerely,

Eva Toby

www.ingramcontent.com/pod-product-compliance
Lightning Source LLC
Chambersburg PA
CBHW042034150426
43201CB00002B/23